BENEATH THE CLOTH

Beneath the Cloth

A collection of poems
by
DONNY BARILLA

Adelaide Books
New York / Lisbon
2020

BENEATH THE CLOTH
A collection of poems
By Donny Barilla

Copyright © by Donny Barilla
Cover design © 2020 Adelaide Books

Published by Adelaide Books, New York / Lisbon
adelaidebooks.org

Editor-in-Chief
Stevan V. Nikolic

All rights reserved. No part of this book may be reproduced in any manner whatsoever without written permission from the author except in the case of brief quotations embodied in critical articles and reviews.

For any information, please address Adelaide Books
at info@adelaidebooks.org
or write to:
Adelaide Books
244 Fifth Ave. Suite D27
New York, NY, 10001

ISBN: 978-1-953510-87-7

Printed in the United States of America

Dedicated to,

The woods where I walk.

Contents

Frock **15**

Bed of My Birth **16**

Winter Night **17**

Sweet Night **18**

Last Sacrament **19**

Pursuance at the End of Day **20**

Speeding Wind **21**

Lone Walk with Lavenders **22**

Madness at the Edge of Night **23**

Wearing the Sleeves of Night **24**

Charms of Night **27**

Bath in the Fog and Cove **28**

From Cloth to Flesh **29**

Service Before Night **30**

Last Meeting **31**

Answers of the Earth   *32*

Alone I Surrender   *33*

Uprooted Path   *34*

Breakfast   *35*

Regaining Youth   *36*

Last Breath of Sweet Winds   *39*

Steam of the Earth   *40*

Peeling the Cloth   *41*

As We Met   *42*

Last Walk   *43*

Rib of the Earth   *44*

Reacquaintance with the Monastery and Field   *45*

Fallen Alabaster Robes   *46*

As the Collar Taps the Floor   *47*

Tucked in the Cool Breath of the Woods   *51*

Cleansing   *52*

After an Endless Moment Alone   *53*

Chasing the Blackbird   *54*

Awaiting Burial and the Fullness of Her Breasts
Which Feed the Earth   *55*

Goblets   *56*

Memories During a Long Walk   *57*

BENEATH THE CLOTH

Remove the Frock **58**

Calgary **59**

Acolyte **60**

Maple Trees **63**

Beyond the Cloister **64**

Foams of the Cove **65**

Looking Back as I Enter the Last of the Woods **66**

Here I Die Alone **67**

In the Garden **68**

Dreaming of the Pond **69**

Reaching Darkness **70**

Suckling from the Wealth of the Earth **71**

Through the Grove **72**

North **73**

Waiting for Harvest **77**

Image I Recall **78**

Gathering Leaves **79**

Past Shadows of Night **80**

Secret **81**

Ashes of the Slithering Clouds **82**

Search **83**

Gardener and the Heat of Summer **84**

Fading Candlelight **85**

As She Lay **86**

As She Lay **87**

Suckling During the Storm **91**

Weeping Earth **92**

Upon the Slope **93**

Jades **94**

Fleece **95**

Dreaming During the Rainstorm **96**

Rendezvous in the Woods **98**

Pinch of Night **99**

Earliest Morning **100**

I Rest in the Shadow **101**

Into the Deep of the Forest Breath **102**

Pearl **105**

Surface of the Earth **106**

Garden Black at Night **107**

We Met at the Pond **108**

Reflection **109**

Exile **110**

Temples *111*

Bloods of the Sky *112*

Darkest *113*

Narcissus *114*

Birth in the Hollow *117*

As I Covet *118*

Upon the Edge of Night *119*

Perched on Mountain Ridge *120*

After the Hike *121*

As the Earth Punishes *122*

Passing the Threshold *123*

Stream in the Meadow *124*

Walking Home *125*

Last Stand *126*

Last Stand *127*

Lost Beneath the Summer Sun *131*

Silence After a Walk *132*

Retreat Upon the Sky *133*

Graves *134*

Mourning Light *135*

About the Author *143*

...from beneath the fibers and threads.

Frock

The full green leaves swelled about the wind as each
curled and wept among the slap of the rain;
sweetly, each found dwelling across the slick clovers of the earth.

I walked across the expanse and reach of the meadow
as the tremble of the sky swept to a distant glen.

Scents of the moist grass filled my lungs with the carvings
of centered oak which filled the wrapping winds, tenderly
I heard the moans of each branch as they sang in the choir
and softened the weeping congregation
of the sweet pasture and field.

I remove the tangling fibers of my nerves and cloth.

Here, I speak of the rise of every perfect
youth and procession of adulthood
which rests on these grasses and bundles
rain upon the leaves and grips
the roots of all taste and swoon.

In the deepest hour if the darkest sky,
I dream of the dusts where I will return
to the fragrance of every twig
and every bud.

Bed of My Birth

I hooked my fingers well into the black,
minerals and deepen into the moisture
of the fragrant bloom of the earth which casts
sweet upon the sweat of the meadow.

I taste myself as I deepen into the clays
and dusty groove where tender
wind drifts, saunters my flesh upon the sweet grip of the sky.

Collars of the wiry branch which reaches
across the wealth of the pond
rips and shreds each fabric of each well stitched ebony garb,
I soothingly take upon the ferns and
mosses which grip to the pond,
full with greens and the darkest blues.

Every stroke of each full patterned kelp
waves as a gushing prayer.

In the dash of a slice of a moment,
I sweeten to the earth and fondle in spades of
the leaf and gathering of nuts and breads
alive in the tender soil of the tender field.

Softly, I walk the silence of the quivering beds of my birth.

Winter Night

The belt of the rings of the moon, softly absorb me in the vapors
of each pinch of the of the dust of my fading shell and flesh.

I hear the echo of the weakening of my bones as the sweat
buckles and slips across the design of my tender skin.

Here, the empty woods walk upon the heavy wind as each stroke
of the fleece of white snow seasons the fullness of my wilted body.

As the gusts of the quiet spread of this cool glaze of the snow mounds
dampen and shake me to the silence of
the hollow of the eager forest,

I sweeten and spread across the masking of
the echoing verbs of the Winter night.

Sweet Night

The apricot and tangerine spread of the perfect sky
wavered and soothed across the silent edge of the earth.

I heard the purr of her sweeping wind as every pause
of her breath, danced eagerly along the softness of my face.

I stepped across the threads of the forest as I listened to the snap
of the branches, whispers of sweet light of the mystic.

Weeping in beads of the mid morning
softness, I waited for the purples,
navies and reds which shroud the chewing clouds of night's sky.

I sweeten to the humming vowels as I recall
the full fragrance of her flesh
which washes across me in burning groins and the mourning
of the event of our death, so fading in pastures
of stones and the heavy blades
of grass and waves of the ferns and reach of the onion grass.

In a moment, I turn and embrace the sky of sweet night.

Last Sacrament

Removing the cloth and hem and stitch from the palest of flesh,
I walk into the deep of the creek as every smooth stone and soot
gathers me in the most tender of droplets from the ash gray sky.

I moan as my legs whimper to the crisp
chill of this spooling gash and a gush of water.

Gingerly, I approach the logs, heavy driftwood, which speak to me
of dancing threads of the shadow and
moments of treasure and charms.

Peering as I reach the swift flood of the river,
I deepen to the sacrament which floods my chest and I quiver
along the wash from which I rose.

Pursuance at the End of Day

Into the fractures of the drip of the hues dampening the blades
well found in the heavy glen,
I savor the breath of the birth of Spring which suckles the Mother
whom fastens across me in vespers and dance.

I feel the tremble of the cool twitch of
my legs and the stir of my groin.

Softly, I find myself in the sweet ices of the frozen pond.
she spoke of the chill of her doughs and bloom of her breasts.

Silently, I shed and roam to her as the vapors dash and dart across
the nakedness of her sweet fragrance and soft aroma,
filling my lungs.

Speeding Wind

Loafing leaves swim loose through the soft winds
cleverly through the cool draft, glazing across the grass beds.

I touch the jam of the earth and look upon
the soil in each patch of clover.

In a moment, I reach to the threads of clouds circling the mountain
and I speak to the thinning air.

I look to the dripping speed and I take to the fastest wind.

Lone Walk with Lavenders

I spoke to you of lavenders which gathered across the moss beds,
stretched and swept.

Each loft of every fragrance pools and
puddles about my feet and softens
my flesh tender as the gentle gloss of gray clouds.

I answer to the blossoms of the Japanese maples.
I place the petal in my palms and wind
took to the mesh of coming night.

With distance, I felt the fangs of darkness swab across me;
I fall to sleeping breath which tangle tender, so I drink
both dew beads and sap from the youngest tree.

Looking upon myself, I witness the smoke
which rises upon the mountain peak.

Madness at the Edge of Night

Morning rain taps upon the black fullness of her hair.
I speak in rhythms as the I strap in cottons and slender denims.

The slapping gusts of wind rob me of my breath and spread
across me, bury me in the mesh of soil,
blood from the bones beneath the earth which slithers gently
and sink upon the scream of the oak.

As I watch, she dredges and slips to the heaviness of the wood.

I remain with the scent of her powders as sulk, fall upon each mud
soaked grass.

With the bloom of this lusty Spring,
I sweep in madness of the tangled branches
of trees of this sultry wood.

Wearing the Sleeves of Night

Leaves upon the branches swept and parted in the carve of Autumn.
I listen to the gasp of sweet nocturnes as I gathered the fragrances
of you and the sweet cream of your tender breasts;

I hear the motions of your palms and fingers as you rise the doughs
and tread near my slender lips.

You speak of the birth of the moans of the tender rib;
she spends her tangled ribbons, disrobes
and sinks upon the falling hush
of coming night.

I face the east which rises to the blood of the burgundy sky.
I feel your arms slither across me and I deepen
to the mud and cake of the meadow.

*I remove these threads and as you look upon
me, slithering in sweat and syrup.*

Charms of Night

I walk to the platform of the mountains edge.
In declaration, I sweep the dust and tan Autumn leaves which
rise sweetly to the fumbling damp winds.

I answer to her fullness and spoke of an old age.

I taste the blood of her heavy breasts and
smelled the rise of quivering dough
as the earth welcomes me in soft departure,
I taste the powders of the quiet lulls which carve me to the slippery
juices of her, trembling upon the edges of my crimping mouth.

I spend every night in the charms of the forest
and I hunt you in bloom and fullness.

Bath in the Fog and Cove

Spices burrowed in the garden wrangled upon the slithering fog,
tender and sweetly alive.

Entering the shroud of the of the quivering pod and bud,
I speak to the tang of the open sky.

Delicate arms slither across the mosses green and the loose leaves
which snare upon the mint, the sweetness of the tomato plants.

Slowly, I take stride to the garden pond and fasten the softest kelp
which waves as a banner across the grip of my sight.

As an opening in the cove upon the ocean reach,
I watch the tender cloth of this man, soaked in curls of the lamb,
I hear the whimper of his flesh as the soot coddles his feet.

I rejoice as the spices sing tender to the dash of the softest sun.

From Cloth to Flesh

I lay the belt, buckle upon the sweet down feather bed and watch
the leaves as they gush upon the treetops
and canvases of the woodlands,
alive with the tiring whispers of this flesh which fills the goblet
with the blood of the earth.

I raise the wine to the edge of my soft lips.
I leave this home and walk upon the silks of the sandy
only to discover the trim curves of the
shadow and dance of the shadow.

Entering the threshold of the crackle and
meshing snare of the heaviest of trees,
I stopped at the growth of the moss and reach of the onion root;
the scents, the incense of the pulse into
this treasure and realm of charms,
I walk upon roots, bog and sprout of the water hemlock.

I return to the sweet flavor of my tender room.
I remove the remaining cloth and wade through
the river in quest of burning flesh.

Service Before Night

She strides through the meadow and fills
herself with fullness of snapping
buds and tender grooves which toss the scents into the blossoms
of the chanting branches of the ivory
petals of this weeping cherry tree.

She motioned to the snapping gust of slumbering winds.

Every slap and snare of the falling sky, she
opened her blouse and leaned
perfectly into the fullest of creams which swell her pale breasts,
open upon the joust of this moaning wind of end of day.

As her feet tamp the stiff blades of the fire
met in the red and orange sky,
she remains poise upon the gleam of this
flickering shout of approaching night.

Last Meeting

Howls of the woods moaned in soft rituals
as the soft bed of the forest and the
scatter of leaves wedged upon the nakedness of my feet.

I met her in the threads of the sounds of
the crows and charms of the finches
which flooded my ears in the nudity of her
fullness and I wept upon the sweet
touch of her in ghosts and vapors which
remove me from this perfect soil.

In a dash of a moment,
I swept to the reach of the treetops and took upon this breeze.

We trembled upon the spruce and angled through the pine.
Upon reaching the meadows, I rest with
her in the cakes of the earth.

Answers of the Earth

I tremble to the voices of the softest winds.
The clovers rejoice in humble manner and cup as a goblet of dew.

I stand alone upon the grass coated hill and gather the sights
of each reaching bud and silent pods;
they burst in pollens, taken to the roaming fields.

I remove my clothing and make love to the answers of the earth.
The pines which gather sparsely, fondly
touch my bloom and whispers;

soothingly, I retrieve the delicate, dashing
bloom of the falling sun.

With the closest of songs and moans of the gentle soil, I
return to the seeds where I lay.

Alone I Surrender

The endless hallways court through the woods.
I enter the grotto and speak soft vowels
to the absence of my ancestors;
silence overcomes me in shards of the falling leaf.

Eager motions of the tender growth of mint,
I weep to the screams of the onion root as
the mourn of the shattering sun
and sweetly I carve into the cakes and
tortes of the loose growth and soil.

I feel my age as the spread of the ground cover suckles upon me.

Uprooted Path

I swim within these clothes,
tangled and sweet as I last with pink with burning flesh.

As I stand upon this quivering meadow,
winds and fragrances of the tender wildflowers dance across me;
I loosen and saute with this heavy cloth
of ebony and slender white.

Upon the edge of the earth, I approach these sands.

Into these legions of gushing water, my lungs with brine,
I soak through these juices of the Mother of this quaking breath,
the cream of the dampening sea.

From feet, thighs, to the burn of my groin,
I sweep my path through the softness of the earth.

Breakfast

Into the delicate, I peer upon the reach of the vast heavens.
I walk through the apricot and tangerine
as the steam rose across the earth.

The sap of the youngest maples speak to
me as I fade to vapors and dust.

The breakfast of daylight soothes as I gently
shadow the fields in dampness
and lulls of the quivering chest.

I hear the sweetest song of the morning dove
and sweet touch of creek and brook
which slithers and answers beneath me.

I feed upon the breast of all which lives and
silence myself to the pulps of the meadow,
forest and dance of the ocean.

I dismiss to the breath of my resurrection as
I return to you in veins of the mesh
of the spirited sky.

Regaining Youth

Into the dark swept regions of the charm of the wood,
I search for the masked pond which stays as floods of life.

After pausing in brevity, I walk this
ancient path and search for every
Treasure and the tender song of the bluebird.

The stream purrs through the gape of these
lulls and angled rocks, boulders;
I breathe the freshest toss of trim of the mint patch.

I sit in the hot spring and fasten every mineral
upon the nakedness of my soothed, heavy flesh.

By nightfall, I vanish and disappear.

*After finding the deep of the wood, I vanish
with the hush of every leaf.*

Last Breath of Sweet Winds

The breads of her swallowed my breath.
Tender, I shook upon the stretch of her swift dancing arms
Which threaded loose upon me.

I hear the tremor of the gusting wind which
pours upon the nearby meadow
And sever each clover and heavy weed.

With scarlet beneath my warming flesh,
The breathe, the scent of the lilac flooding from your hair
As you shed your petals upon the bed where I sleep,
Lost in the fullness of these pollen filled fields.

With the shadow of night, these spears of grass tangle me in chords
As I fade to the roaming stretch of your sweet winds.

Steam of the Earth

Standing, I reach as the dark wood of the thick of the forest.
Winds slap through the canvas top of
the trees, hustle of these leaves.

I wander, lost upon the sleek wrap of the moss covered rocks;
I fill my lungs, mouth, with the steam of the earth.

By night, I cloak in shadow and darkness.
By day, I shrouded in shadow and darkness.

I wiped the endless sweat from the loitering edges of my flesh.

Heavy dome of the ash gray of the sky tamped
as a rash, burning upon the soils,
Stretch of the tempest uncoiled upon the weeds.

Waiting for the precious moment when I
slumber upon the last and longest
Breath, I perch upon the fallen fogs and rest upon the savory mud.

Peeling the Cloth

Against the passions of your warm breasts,
I quiver at the lips and suckle every
grain of the floods of the flush
of the galaxy which wraps around us.

I peel your cloth as buds open in the hour of Spring.

Sweet fragrant softness upon this growth and this full earth,
I smell the scent of the angles of human pulse and eager moans
from bed to lofting pollens.

Taking you with me in the dripping
fullness of the stains of lusty April,
you speak to me in riddles of the bloom of the sultry meadow
which soothes the nudity of my feet.

With the drip of the burgundy sun as
each pause and dash of evening,
I turn to the threads as they unravel from your eager bones.

As We Met

Trimmed, the rows of maize thread and reach the forest edge.
I sleep upon this floor, the pines howling in to the winds
as the descending sun fragments shadows
upon the empty stalks.

Rising at the hour of sweet darkness,
I step in certainty upon the pinecones
and layers of the needled bed,
spreading across the woods.

I declare to the bark and branches which relish the cool breeze
courting across the hills and distant rise of the mountains,
sauntering chips of ice soothe the crimp and death of the buds.

I find you on a mountain ledge and
hook my fingers into your soil.
I speak to you of the fade of your jasmine breath as the lavenders
reach with their last push and quiet declaration.

I taste your flesh upon the eager wind and
fondle upon my return to the Wintery
rows of Autumn harvest.

Last Walk

Upon this stride through the fields of somber wheat,
tender, I soothe in vapors and trellising fog.

Looking above, the wind scurries and pulls me as the petal
of the cherry blossom, pursed in my palm.

I listen to the blood beneath the earth and
screams of the bone and quivering flesh
which Fade as I look upon the juices of the passing creek;
well into the majesty of the tug and soft
touch of each mountain reach
lulling upon the clothing of every falling cloud,
I return and weep beads of pearls as joy trembles in my chest.

Rib of the Earth

The scalps of the sleek boulders and jettison
rocks softened with the threads
of the mosses and the dance of each wavering fern.

Now, in the smashing hour of Spring, I rest
against the triumph the sycamore tree,
so quietly, I wait for the breath of her to warm my ivory flesh.

Standing, I gather my things and tread
to the chilled gushing creek
which harbors life into the quiver of my parchment throat.

Rested, I burrow into the caverns of the
mausoleum of this woodland grove.

I look upon the softness of my cooled flesh and moaning bones
as the rib of the earth pampers her to greet me.

Reacquaintance with the Monastery and Field

With humid warmth in my breath, I loafe upon
the stone floor, walls and saturate in my stew and salve.

Standing on the height of the highest
grooves of the ancient home,
I peer, sting my sight across the tans and
light browns of the open field.

With the lustre of the wavering stalks,
I disrobe and swarm, cascade the sweet dance of the lusty threads
which once would soothe my nakedness upon the breeze.

Now, I suckle the saps, carried across in the floods across my flesh,
which tremble each fiber of my thin silky hair, I coat in the wash
of this perfect wind.

Fallen Alabaster Robes

I wept beads of the sweet taste of the earth
as I trembled and coiled, tangled cloth and
stain upon the alabaster threads.

I motion my leather face and stretch my
full, open arms as I embrace the end
of the day and approach bitter sweats of
the blisters of the blackest soil.

Near, upon the branches of the oak tree,
a swift, crying murder of crows absorbs the
softness of this approaching meat
which dashes across the winds, returned in dusts.

These breasts of the rolling hills milk the dance of the tender breeze.

I soften and soothe the full nakedness of our
sultry bodies and walk upon the creams
which feed and send me to the bridge of
every spooling creek and slowly
I rest in the massive sea which treads my sight
upon the edge of the dusty earth.

As the Collar Taps the Floor

Looking upon her, I felt the cloth, threads,
stitches and hems loosen
as the slender part of her lips opened the collar and softly
her mouth parted as the flourish and
part of these trembling buds;
I recall first glance upon her perfect flesh
which danced as the sweats
slipped across the pale shadows of each breast.

My hands cherished to goblets as the sulking press of her gown,
swollen in the shades of night, I covet
the fullness of her milk filled
satchels and I tremor upon the shattered
blunders of her shaken vows.

Beneath the shades and hustling silvers of the moonlight,
I deepen upon the slices and valleys where each
broom and butler shred the sap of the morning bloom;
pale creamed yellows of the sun shakes each crimping palm
as the shroud of our flesh quivers across the cool stone floor.

I fade from this chapel and return to the dust of my brethren.

Tucked in the Cool Breath of the Woods

She stood, angled by the creek and scatterings of the ponds,
Removing stitches and loosening her blouse which cascaded across
The stiff joust of the tall grasses as she bathed in the crisp waters
Which paused upon her nudity and fullness.

She moaned to the heat of Summer as the dashing sweat
Glistened across her temples and she dipped to the edge
Of her neck and softened the warmth which ran through her breasts
And trembled in sauces of the burn of her groin.

Leaves, the pages of the tale of these antiquated trees, tossed
Across the sweet dance of the riveting stream as winds scurried
Across the charms and palaces of these tender woods.

Leaving the bloom of the Summer woods,
She stepped across the threshold where field met a flood of trees.

A flock of starlings dashed across the
trembling hush where the fog
Dripped and soothed the emeralds of the earth.

Upon the mesh of the open fields, cloth
clung to the moisture of her cool
Dripping flesh;
Every bird spoke to her as she swam through
the threads of the deepening sky.

Cleansing

Rocks spread across the river banks, jagged and perched as teeth,
soft bleach of the sun, I edged in the ivory
of the slicing passage of water
which tunneled through the soot and dancing kelp.

I wash the ages of corrosion from the soils of the cloth which
threaded through the hermetic dance of a heavy wood.

Upon the grotto, hollow of the courtship of the gnarled forest,
softly, the sun soothed every stitch of the thinning robe.

After an Endless Moment Alone

I reached my hands to the seam of the slicing creek
which hosted the patterned spread of moss and nearby soot.

Softly, the sweet vowels of the songbird opened upon the cool
spooling breath of the tender sky.

Washing the sweat and patches of caked mud which lay across
the weariness of my whimpering skin,

I bathe into the quick slapping dance which
moistens both thighs and groin.

Last moment of the shadow of my darkest night,
I slept along the trunk and felt the scatter of each branch
as the tumble of the pine needles which coat me across my
whisper which trembled across my tongue, I spoke to the dance
where I loosened upon the fog covered ground.

Chasing the Blackbird

I hear the octaves of the swoon of the blackbird.
Groans of the winds which chant sweetly as a choir
which woos me and I follow the dashing
flavors of the wild mint, honey,
and scream of the onion root.

Well into the next moment, I swell upon the floods of the bog
as all became silent and tender marsh pressed
eager upon my legs and hips.

Sweat spread across me and the heavy howling call of night
deepened me into the flash of the cave of my pumping blood.

After calling upon you, I softened and sank
upon the tremble of your breasts.

Awaiting Burial and the Fullness of Her Breasts
Which Feed the Earth

I stood well planted upon the arcs and calluses of my heavy feet;
removal of these robes, I wavered and found the lusty breath
of the spooling sky which danced across my
weakening body and aging flesh.

By the gasp of morning's freshest tumbling toss,
the red maple, the webbing branches
of the sycamore, I watched as she slept upon the jades and emeralds
of the Autumn spread.

The slipping blouse and fumbling skirt
opened her in quivering waves
which tossed her fragrances upon me and calmly, the food
of her milk pressed breasts swept sweetly
to the scent of every dying bud.

By the dancing tremble of the perfect evening hour,
I soak beneath the soil and listen to the
scuffing leaves which honor me
fast into a procession of this dying earth.

Goblets

Upon the levelled ground, well into the slippery fields,
I look upon the basin and threshold of the cranberry sky.

Sweetly, I taste the pastes and milks of the goblet of your
Tender breasts which covet each seed and bud scouring across
The meadow which leads to the coddling twigs and branches
Of the shuddering woods.

I listened to the shout of the darting
charm as finches opened across
The smooth ivory sky.

I answer the call of the field, sky, and lusty forest
While phantoms of the death of pastures of the torte,
Well burrowed into the cake of the earth,
I tremble and soothe the glazes
Of the freeze of the Autumn moss.

By the messages of the scampering birds, I
Spoke upon the fullness of your body which
spread across the heavy earth.

Memories During a Long Walk

Placed upon the edge, ridge of the forest and
field, I witnessed the mesh of the branches,
shedding the white bark of the white birch,
swiftly, I stood at the threshold
of the cove, leading into the woods and
remained open beneath my frock.

I removed both glands and regal rod as
the heavy wind glazed promise
to me.

I sank into the willow and cedars of the
trembling woods as every snapping bud
opened and cloaked upon a petal of a cherry tree and I softened
the gate of the coddle and triumph as I burn upon you.

Now, the deepest moaning crackle of
dead trees showered in the dust
of their own, I sulked upon the youngest
of flesh and returned to where
I gently came.

Remove the Frock

A flood of dust layered across the meadow and tenderly,
I walked through the sheets of necessary rain and morning droplets
of each quivering clover which cups the pearls of dancing dew.

Meeting her on the high eager slope,
I feel the pulse of her as I feel the pulse of this thickening earth.

As I swam through the seasons which
adjusted in shades of the patterns
of rain, sweet fibers and hems of this cloth,
I bed upon the grave of endless
leaves and gently, I swabbed my parchment throat.

Together, I tremble at the sauces of my heavy mouth and lips
with the sauntering wind, soothing, calming me to the visceral
blood and amber shades of this falling sky.

I place her trim shadow and pale ripeness
which awakens from the breasts
of her as I swell to the gems of her sweetest waist.

Calgary

After removing myself from every edge and corner
of the linens, down and roam of the quilt,
I awaken to the sauces of life
and slither upon the dark hour as the
resist of the rise of humble gloss
seasons across me and by the strike of
the chapel, trembling in each
metallic clang, I coddle you in preference,
the peal of the orchid.

Now, resting, I swim in the entanglement of the endless glisten
of the cross and beads which sweetly rest
upon the nakedness of the palest
flesh which moans for the charge of the mount
where I remove my dampness and further upon the pastures
which soften and grip every corner and nook,

The moaning sky tosses a tempest upon the ebonies which I wear.

Acolyte

Upon the smallness of you, I weep through the realms of Autumn
which unfold as the clothing of night,
shed upon the wide open bed.

We gather the maple leaves and by afternoon,
light the fire which warms
us in the woods and tenderly, I lay my hands
upon the supple nape and nave.

As I swoon upon the thick, rigid cloth which shadows as the velvets
of fallen night.

I place you upon my lips and enter the grove where I last witnessed
the bones and sweet marrow, alive and
soothing the crimp of the earth.

I speak to you in tremors which unfurl and
wrestle the denims and fine white shirt
which gathers about the woodland floor.

I awake and look upon the spread of the floor which gushes
tossing dusts through the wealth of the air.

Walking beneath the full redness of the sky, I lost my way.

Maple Trees

From quivering lips and the throbbing beat well within her chest,
I absorbed the fall of her habits as each
flutter of each full, silk thread
of hair danced upon the carry of the wind.

Swift, I took her palest spread of her smooth
skin and moaned upon the fragrances
which soothingly escaped the fullness of her body.

I clutch the dampness of the meadow where we walked.

As we lay upon the glisten of the grotto,
where mosses lulled upon us,
I softened upon the doughs of her breasts.

Walking home, the purification and benediction of the rain
fell upon the drizzle of the blood which
stirs in the veins beneath our flesh.

Into the breach of this perfect, warmth of the thigh and groin,
I smelled the sap of each perch of each of the maple trees.

Beyond the Cloister

Morning dew, glistening as the diamonds of
the pouches of weed, clover and grass,
I walked with naked feet and stopped,
knelt by the brook as the soft wind
pampered and coddled me in touch and scent.

Having left the great, towering, stone house,
I removed the sweet passions
of the billowing incense and discovered the mint as each stretch
swept upon the nudity of my ankle and heel.

I relish in the mumble of the trellising gush of the perfect water.
I traced my fingers upon the sweat of my fine,
thin hair and drew each motion of sap
as I removed every stitch of clothing and
fumbled upon the gathering of trees
and eagerly, I smelled the flavors of the honey,
suckled in the sweetness of the hive.

Entering the dash of the approach of night,
I softened upon the cool breeze and tenderly, I filled my lungs
with the touch of this Autumn night.

I reach the highest perch and look upon the vast
expanse of the meadow and slithering path.
I catch sight of the cloister and chants
trembling across the valley.
gently, I turn and walk away.

Foams of the Cove

Alive with the dust which settled upon the silence of my shroud,
softly, the fine scent of the settling grass swept across the heaviness
of my bones and moisture of the earth thickened upon my marrow,
the peel of my flesh.

Here, the posture of the greatness of this towering oak,
carvings of the moss and shaking branches, winds meddled
into the blooming buds which burst at every arrival, I
stew upon the sauces which sink deeply
through the pastes of the rock and mud.

Now, light of the fracture of this salt of the wind,
this flood of the open cove of the sea buries
the dust of my frock and tenderly,
eons past, I sweep upon the trembling foams.

Looking Back as I Enter the Last of the Woods

The forest path, riddled in stitches of the earth,
tossing Autumn leaves across the woodland
floor, I open my shirt and tremble
as the scurry of the humble breeze, I take the fresh dancing wind
and deplete among the fastening soil which
hugs every ridge of every boot.

I feel the thrash of my chest and softly, I
slumber upon the grooves of the earth.

With the sight of her fallen robes and glazes of her nudity,
every moving carve upon the earth moans
across me in thinning hair and age
of the thickening lusts which spread
from me as I sink to the clay
and fattening mud of the depth of the woods.

Here I Die Alone

As the crumbling shadow of the darkening sky loosens
and the fittings of clothing and threads which tore, I
Soak upon the smashing rains which
soak into the sting of my flesh.

With the glaze of the holly bush which
holds the dew pearls, suspended
Upon the grooves of the leaves, I tremble
at the veins and curling cups.

By the edge of nightfall, I slip in the
slumber of the satchel of the earth,
Winds thrash and by the deepest moment of night,
I hear the fade of the distant church as I soak upon the smooth
Threading waters of the tamp of the soil.

Upon removal of the cloth I once wore,
the croon and wooing clang
Of the death of the chapel, slowly, I fade upon the dust.

In the Garden

I loafe through the garden of perfect and fine spices,
quivering at the sweet breath of the wind which stirs
the fragrances, well spread and upon me.

The breadth of the soil pampers tenderly in yeasts and silent
transitions of the decay of myself and my
brotherhood and fellowship.

With the tap of the silence of the needling rain,
I swell the growth where the sap of the
open majesty of the towering tree,
I softly sleep in this humble dance, coiled
with the fever of the warming of my flesh.

Dreaming of the Pond

The pond soothed as the spread of cool
flesh dampening across my fullness.
I shook beneath the quivering branches of the elm; soft
maples wavered each leaf which swooned across me as a fan.

I removed the thin cottons of my clothing
and dredged into the crisp
waters as every fiber of every hair cloaked across my face and scalp.

Resting in the nudity of my slithering
flesh which slide the sweet winds
across me, I witnessed the warmth of my
bloods flush through my veins.

I awoke in the jester of morning and tenderly
I looked upon her as she slept curled
and poise; I watched her smile quiver across her
lips as she loafed her black hair across
her palest of pigments of her skin.

Reaching Darkness

Beyond the frontier of the last of this glistening emerald wood
which drew moisture from the layer of these lowering clouds,
I tap the edge of my tongue and tasted the minerals of the earth.

Upon feeling my last tangling breath
which filled my chest with fumes,
steam and flickering fog, dancing across
the leaves and pebbles and stones,
I angled to the deep of the trembling
earth and slept in the most majestic of crouch and curl.

I looked last to the creamed yellows and
burgundies of the fading sky at dusk.
with sight poised upon the peach of her skin,
I sank upon each pocket of dust,
slippery cakes which swab me to the flank of darkness.

Suckling from the Wealth of the Earth

Swollen clouds filled the sky in shades of ash as the dew
fastened beneath my feet.

I swallowed every breath of morning and wept
to the defeat of shrouded darkness.
So early, the charm of the sweetest
finches trembled across the sky.

Stopped at the lavender bush and soft
songs of the nearest willow,
I edged closer to the rising sun.

Tenderly, I leave the cloth of the longest
slumber and tempt the skin
which roams the earth as fibers of dust reflects
across my skin and nakedness.

Secretly, I taste the milk of the breasts of the earth;
I spool upon the madness of the sweetest
fragrance of this burning, warming life.

Through the Grove

I walk through the thick of the apple grove
and dance upon the peeling
brightness of the sweet trembling sky
which hosts the shades of the sun;
there gasps endless hues of the disrobing
fleece from breasts to thighs.

Next, I enter the needled fabrics of the
empty woods and gingerly
I hear the moans of the silent
Autumn leaves and the approach of the sting of Winter.

Placed by the secrets of the gushing creek,
I sweat into the cloth I soak within
as each probe of the sun casts the longest
shadows, tempting the nudity
of this sulking mounds of leaves and
fallen branches. By nightfall
I chill upon my lusts which snap as the
teeth across the skin of the fruit.

North

Walking across the stitches of the long,
dusty path which scurried
as a tamp of dust,
I trembled into the moaning clash of every rustle of the leaves.

I wade through the spines of the smallest of creeks and the coolest
of water which I drank as the pebbles softened my feet.

By the last reign of nightfall, I felt the sweat of my thickened skin
cool and glide across every bead and removal of cloth.

Now, I stand on top of the highest mountain,
this smooth mountain peak
which shrugged my sight across the pale, dusty boulders.

Fading in this swift dancing moment, I
loosen with the eager breath,
lofting in particles and fibers along the northern wind.

I dance among the faded leaves.

Waiting for Harvest

I slither across the frailty of the nakedness
of her soft, trembling skin
and the rapture of her bones which spoke
from the grasses and spread
where she slumbered into the pie and torte of this coveting earth.

As I stood, my swift, keen eyes scoured the most distant fields
and beyond, the endless colors tangled
from leaf to adjoining leaf.

A cool wind smashed across my chest and
bust which harbored the thudding
slips of my heart as I eagerly fall to the tender taste of the field.

Well into the perfect hour of Spring, I
carved my bones and loosened
skin as the grass coils across me and I speak of the next harvest.

Image I Recall

I step on this collection of emerald colored moss as the sweat
of the trees and limbs of the trees shed droplets upon me.

I marvel at the softness of the gusting wind and tenderly
the branches loosen and fumble across the green carpeted soil.

Reaching the patch of clover, sweet fibers
and pollens fill the vacancy
of my chest as the near groupings of mint sharpen my voice as I
call upon the descension lowering clouds.

As I watch the swabbing douse of rain,
the canvas of the treetops
smack heavily.

I delve into the deepest shroud of the
woodland and quivering hyacinths
reach sweet, I find her figure spread across the hollow as the light
slaps across the floor and speaks of her in the finest intimacy.

Gathering Leaves

The maples thrashed each branch across the scattered gatherings
as the browns and scarlet leaves loosened from bark and twig.

Arrival of Autumn cast loafing beams of near twilight
through the pink fleece of the sky.

Gently, I walked through the piles of shredded parchment;
each October scent wavered over me in this tender fleece.

With whipping winds, I listened to the
screams of the lulling, lowering
clouds.

In the fraction of the most eager moment, I softly thought of you
as you once would toss both blouse and skirt.

Past Shadows of Night

Glamor of every shard and glass, stings with
loafing aroma amd wooden pew
which creaks as fellowship hustles across the marble floor.

Walking the narrow asphalt which stretches from edge to edge,
skies swell and release a heavy dash of rain.

I speak of cleansing fragrance which taps
across me and the sweetest
tread of swelling into the cluttered sidewalk and grass.

She spoke to me of touch and nudity as
the thin stretch of her cotton
shirt pasted to the milk filled breasts which
loosened and swept with moisture.

By the break of morning, my brain swims
with humid pangs deepening across
the brown panelled room.

Secret

I enter you and discovered the secret of the woods.
Into the deep of the gnarled branches and the
scattered films upon the tremble of the pond,
a single leaf falls and rivets the murky water
in spreads of circles and splashing
eddies upon the tender grass.

Asleep at the pebbles and ferns and moss, echoes of the moaning
light of dawn, I hear the voices of the endless choir of my brethren
as the silence of the surrounding sky swells upon me.

The trees speak of every bud and the
snapping pop of pods and glistening
perches where the pearled beads of flickering water fall upon me.

Every spread of every gush and rippling cascade of soft water,
I suckle upon the swabbing foams of the stream and so tenderly
you place my mouth upon your breast
and hands upon your thighs.

Following the courting creek, the cove opens
upon the wealth of the ocean.
Gold yellows glisten across the horizon as
water and buoy dance upon the sweet
breath of brine and sandy stroke.

Ashes of the Slithering Clouds

Black ashes of the low slithering clouds
swept across me as the leaves
curled and spoke to the passion of the
swelling torrents, born of the
latest evening which flickers each stitch of my cloth.

As each scourge of each slapping rain pounds the land before me,
I feel the earth soften as the oldest leather which loosens across
the fabric of time.

I reach the clutter of these Autumn woods.

Sitting upon the fallen log which pensively
speaks to me of dancing branches
which impregnates into the deep of the
earth, I lean upon the nearest tree
and sleep against the terror of the sulking pasture and heavy
sighs which tremble the edges of my ears and face.

Search

Across the quivering fields of wheat, I court
through the trim of the edges
and soothingly,
I spread my arms as the stalks threads
through my fingers and hands.

Tender slopes and curves which travel and
muscle upon the ache of my feet,
reach with rocky soil, eager dusts blooming
across the spread of these denims
and aging boots, I fill myself with the breath of the slouching sky.

The pink and thick merlot of the sky
fattens the shade from the nearness
of the gated threshold of the pamper of the
madness of these deepening woods.

I pause at the curvature of the bow of opened
trees and gingerly, I thought of you.

Gardener and the Heat of Summer

I awoke to the depression of the down feather bed
which slung glimmering particles of dust across pillows,
throughout the room.

I carried the scent of her so deeply into the clamor
of the corners of my lungs and soothed the sauces of her across
every press and slope of my pale burrowing body.

With strands of chestnut hair, stuck against my temples and neck,
tenderly, I dreamt upon the smooth, repetitive breezes
as my finger sulked across the soil and mulch.

Tenderly, she fades upon the gust of the evening winds.

Fading Candlelight

Upon suspension of the corners of the bed,
I harvest the sloping curves of your body and
breath the fragrance of your wrists
and neck.

With the soothing breeze flooding through
the sliver of the open window,
the threads of the black cloth which penetrates my flesh
sends aromas across the room and sweetly I place the softness
of my mouth upon the cream filled breasts.

These shadows of night flicker and dance across the walls,
crimp the fading candlelight as the room so gingerly
crowds every stitch in darkness.

I awaken in coils as I hear the thrusting
echoes of the chapel bells.
The dome of the sky bled in burgundies and slice of the peach.

As She Lay

Screams which thrust and echo across the meadow fill myself
with the chatter of every tree, sparse
across the width and breadth
of the fields where she lay.

I remove a single maple leaf and fondly
look upon the veins of every crimp
and the curl of the edges which humbly await the rain.

The floods sweetly delve into the ridges
of the soft mud of the pasture;
again, the branches quiver and crack
the lumber which eagerly lays
upon the earth.

I witness the blue lights of the slaughter of the sky.
here, I walk knee deep in the joust of the
stalk and reach of the onion sprout.

Next to a moment before nightfall, I
discover a swelling pond and look
upon myself as the mud and breads of the earth tangle across me.

In a sudden flash, I see her naked in the heaviest of rains.
Here, I recall the flight of the mourning dove.

As She Lay

Screams which thrust and echo across the meadow fill myself
with the chatter of every tree, sparse
across the width and breadth
of the fields where she lay.

I remove a single maple leaf and fondly
look upon the veins of every crimp
and the curl of the edges which humbly await the rain.

The floods sweetly delve into the ridges
of the soft mud of the pasture;
again, the branches quiver and crack
the lumber which eagerly lays
upon the earth.

I witness the blue lights of the slaughter of the sky.
here, I walk knee deep in the joust of the
stalk and reach of the onion sprout.

Next to a moment before nightfall, I
discover a swelling pond and look
upon myself as the mud and breads of the earth tangle across me.

In a sudden flash, I see her naked in the heaviest of rains.
Here, I recall the flight of the mourning dove.

I hear the shattering of the chapel bell.

Suckling During the Storm

I waver to the width of her waist and the breadth of her thighs,
the breadth of her meaty, milk filled breasts.

I lean upon the softness of her shoulder and weep
to the rain which taps outdoors upon patio
and sulks from the eaves.

I reach the curling crimp of my palm and
rest every stretching finger upon
the doughs of her full torso.

Slumber upon the patio, I look to the treads
and smash of the opening sky
as ebony threads blow across me in torrent and tempest.

The sweeping joust of the screams of the sky,
each grass blade folded upon the smack
of the sauces of each winded blend, I saunter
into the fullness of her, loosening
of the blouse and smoothest of hands
drape across my thin, blonde hair.

The afternoon sun sliced through the black and
grays swelling of the dome of the sky.
I deepened into her full arms.

Weeping Earth

I felt the thudding crimson which flooded through his veins.
The creek spooled through the fields
surrounding this wooden home
as I knelt and drank with parchments in my throat.

I paused as I witnessed him remove the stitch of his cloth.
I slithered through the open window
and the crack of the patio door.

Climbing, I drenched the opened mouth
and the fullness of his lungs
as he buckled to the weakness of his knees.

Tenderly, I boiled the threading bloods
which weakened and gripped him
to the heaviness of his fallen arms, legs and quivering torso.

With a thrust to the lowering grays of this dome of the sky,
I loosen and fasten upon this quaking mercy and
salts which relish in the deep of the cove
of the sea which gathers me in the
moisture of the weeping earth.

Upon the Slope

I relish in the clench of her touch and stretch,
softly the satins of her blouse and grip of this skirt,
I swept and angled my heavy flesh upon
her as the touch of her thin lips
drew milk from every satchel of bounty.

I took the crimp and smallness of her delicate hands as the bloom
of the winds, fondling upon the meadow, I unfasten the buttons
and tossed her quivering skin, bones and they shook in rapture
as the softness of this flesh, prickled and served.

By morning, she vanished and left the
dance of her scent and fragrance.
I wandered every field in tossing and wash
of the jousting blade and spears.

With smash and spreading blood upon the slope where she slept,
I turn and fall upon the descension of the trees and slicing roots.

Jades

With naked feet, I walked upon the cupping
dash of the cupping clovers
as the mint patch swell and groomed
across me, alive in the threads
of the Autumn leaves, tugging across the tan, sculpted fields.

Well beneath the clay and mud of the
stretching greens of the earth,
I quiver to the moans which shake upon
the pale bones of the ancient grave.

I whisper of the marrow which trembles
across the rain puddles and I
drink upon the quick forming ponds, field
spread, I bled upon the bloom
of the twitch of the leaf.

With the rise and bloom of nightfall, I
sulked upon the jades of the earth.

Fleece

I shook the icicles from my tangled beard
and stepped upon the soft
white fleece.

Walking into the fields as the sloping, sulking
branches loosened every pinecone
and the crowds of the needle floor.

Now, so deeply quivering into the freeze of
the endless meadow and pasture,
I lull upon the ice of this earth.

Dreaming During the Rainstorm

I slouched upon the bench, the eaves cascaded
over me as the puddles gathered
and swiftly the heavy, warm wind wrapped
across the chill of my face and neck.

Pressing my way along the cobblestone path,
I stay, soaked and trembling as
I reached the street, hosting every smack of pebble and rain.

I thought of the rigid clothing and the perfect
collar as the belt unwound upon the
bedroom floor.

Lush and foamed with salted rains from the
sea bed and shoreline, so close to the
smash of the chapel, I looked to the
thrashing rains as they subsided

And tenderly, I found him holding me in the
coarse rigid hands which softly stroked
the paleness of my thighs.

The rain dashed for the stretch of the orange
and navy colored sky as I placed

BENEATH THE CLOTH

my supple hands upon the wedge and growth
of his gentle thighs and trembling groove
of the penis which covers me in pale cloaks.

The shore and the boasting sounds of the
sea, faded with the awakening sauces
where I slumbered alone and danced into the grooves of
the sidewalk and sprouts between the
cracks of the asphalt and stone.

Rendezvous in the Woods

I found her in the deepest tangle of the woods.
she listened to the verbs of the open branch
and the moan of each thrashing leaf.

She peeled her clothing as a snap of a fertile, lusty bud
which shed pollen across the Autumn breeze and the moisture
of the softest soil upon the earth.

I placed my hands along the shadowed
edge of her pale white breasts.

She met me here in nudity and buried her slender, cool fingers
across the edge of my groin as the wild,
wind cast a gathering of leaves
gently upon us and we slept beneath the
quilt of the maple and elm.

I enter the home, dwelling where the air
lingers stale and the windows
rattle upon every smack of the uprising wind.

I reach in my pocket and remove a burgundy leaf.
gently, I place it upon the table where the words blend and fade.

Pinch of Night

Endless, I look upon the steps from my
heavy feet as I fasten my eyes
upon every step, stop and groove.

From the palest pigment and hue worn deeply within her flesh,
her swell and bloom of her listless thinning hair, I
place two coins upon the caves of her eyes.

I weave my way across this grass field
and feel my legs deepen across
the emeralds of the edge and basin of the trunk of the tree.

The sun bleaches the fields and burns me in
the wrath of the crisp, clay earth.

By the pinch of night, I lose my breath upon the gasping wind.

Earliest Morning

Quivering leaves coiled and threaded to the passing breeze
as each snapping stem loosened and sent
the crimping parchments across
the scurry of the wind.

I fell upon the dust and tender soils of the rigid earth.

She spoke to me from the rib she bloomed and blossomed from
as every curve of her sweet flesh taunted me into her full bosom
and the powdered paleness of the temptation
from which she slouched.

The snap of the red skinned flesh quivered
across her teeth as the chymes
of the winds, crackling branches, I witnessed
the stews upon her head, hair full
of sweat and the tossing leaves rustle in temptations of the beads
tapping upon the coarseness of the earth.

I tossed upon the waist, thighs and fullness
of her cream filled breasts.
I rest with the fall of the palest yellow sun.

I Rest in the Shadow

Past the lingering fog which slipped across the forest deep,
I walked, trembled upon my shaking feet and
rose to the top of this mountain path.

Mist pressed upon the paleness of my
skin and moistened my chestnut
hair.

I looked upon the quivering spread of
cottons as every curve opened my
waist and thighs as the mountain clouds shook
as the perfection of her trembling
body and waist.

Resting upon the highest boulder, the
highest peak, I lean along the stretch
of this triumph of the sycamore as I loosened
my breath into the thin air of night.

I slid to the base of the smoothest boulder and gathering rocks.
with a moment shaking the shadow of nightfall, I dipped through
the pastures of trembling night.

Into the Deep of the Forest Breath

I held the curl and crimp of his palm in the
width and breadth of my palm.
Upon breathing the sweet fragrance of his fine yet full hair,
we walked across the field and listened to
the cracking clang of the chapel bell.

His eyes peered across the blush of the falling Autumn leaves
as he walked knee deep in the joust of
the speared jade green grass.

As we reached the deep of the trim lined threshold
where the forest opened and bloomed
across the trembling oak and the stroke
of the pine coves and maples,
I took him into the black, humid breath of the forest.

The sky shook upon us and the trembling
breath soaked upon the lingering breath.

I quiver to the darkest shade of black.

Pearl

Pearl dew beads glisten on the edge of
grass blades and cup of the clover.
Softly, I stand on top of the green grass, on top of the hill,
I descend to the dip of the valley and rest upon the slithering creek.

The sky swelled with dampness and shed
the heavy grays and spooling black
which loosened smashing rains upon the sweet taste of the earth.

With the fullness of my chestnut brown hair, gushing water
pasted across my scalp and every contour
of my body and eagerly I drank
every fresh swallow.

Hours past, the threads of the ripe yellow sun
warmed me with the coat of the quilt,
my flesh pronounced as blankets which turned
the saturation into heat and cottons.

Within this moment, I stood upon the
maple trees and tenderly, I recall
the removal of your cloth and cottons
which fell upon the sweet bloom
of the lull where this breeze thickens in recollection.

Within the damp slumber of night, I
swell and hold the girth of you
as we once would.

Surface of the Earth

I address each moment with a pause, then I covet the blackness
sweeping across the surface of the earth.

Streams which foam in ivory white slap
across my feet and gingerly
I smooth the skin and stroke the winded hair
of you as I place my soft cupping palms
across the palest of eager thighs.

Along the deep where the chapel bell
stings every slope of the earth,
I hear the whimper and moan from the frailty of his mouth.

I reach the films of the satin of the sheets
which stretch upon the dome
of the sky.

He quivers beneath me as each tender muscle and tendon swabs
across the pigment of the approach of the shining day.

Garden Black at Night

I bathe naked in the greens and suckling creeks of the garden
as tender dew and sleek polish floods across the sloping hills.

Upon touching the tremble of her tender, sweet flesh of her
perfect abdomen, rains fell across us and the dash of the gazelle.

Her fragrance swelled across the pine trees and cascaded the edge
of my mouth and deeply into the deep hollow of my lungs.

The breads of her fruitful breasts motioned and pause at the tip
of my tongue and eagerly I rose to the softest, palest powders
which drenched from thighs to the cave of her buried seeds.

Into the fine silks of our slumber,
I coiled across her and sank the edges of
my ivory teeth along the passages
of every soft triumph as the winds hurried and
the clouds drew forth, painted black.

We Met at the Pond

I wept across the cracks on the marble slab as tender
strokes of wind swabbed across me and the tickling grass
wavered and thumbed my ankles which ached and shook.

I walked endless along this pebbled and dusty road
which threaded as the coil of a spine; lofting breath
from the smack of the bells, I shrouded myself in rhythms
of the surmounting rain.

I smiled at him and looked upon the childish lines of his face
as the blonde of his blossoming hair fell
across the shoulders and sleeves.

I retrieved my lusts, buried in the deep stretch of the meadow
as sweet wildflowers tossed every fragrance into the slithering
bloom where I last looked upon you.

You wade through the murky, heavy greens of the pond
as I removed the pants and shirt covering every inch and stitch
I wore.

At the darkest hour of night, I recovered
against the thunder of the bells.
I removed the heaviness of my step. Tamp along the meadow
which I returned with to drenched, tears of the earth.

Reflection

Crimson blades speared across the full pink, sweeping below.
Slowly, I walked the woodland path as
every shade of green leaves
shook the raindrops as each gathered across my feet.

Further into the gnarled depth of the darkening forest,
I listened to the passages as the song of this bardic rhythm,
thrusting dance of the belly dancer as the trembling tree branches
shook every bud and pod.

By the charms of night I fell upon the dash of the darkest canopy
as the moon tried so eagerly to wedge and plunge.

By morning, I drew sap from the maple and scurried, roamed lost
in the travels of this velvet stroke of the warmth of the sky.

I proclaimed my seething moans as the soaked black legs and torso
breathed swiftly across my ears.

In turn of the dance of the showering
leaves, I shook and lost my way.

Exile

I fell upon the hot clays of the earth and
felt the absence coil through
the empty air as the sky fell with blues
and motioned each cloud across
the width of the horizon.

Pounding bloods in the thin stretch of these
veins, I recall his frailty and the cup
of his small, loose palm.

In the swift breath, I absorbed the fragrance
of his fine hair and the soft
tremble of his glistening thighs which I
heard in the fade of my ears.

I leaned against the oldest oak and delved
into the swift sky as the darkness
swabbed and coddled across me.

Temples

I press my lips across the curve of your soft, gentle neck;
the moisture of the sweat which rolls along the grooves
of your temples saturates the edge and tip of my tongue.

I deepen my hand with the cupping
goblet of my palm and sweetly
I tap upon the rigid dance and fumbling creams as the warmth
of the pounding sun floods us in the
distance of stretching shadows.

I look upon the meadow where I dwell;
the unforgiving shroud of darkness cools the beads of sweat
as I return to the sulking church from where I pattern and devise.

Bloods of the Sky

The sky opened as the vein above the earth and softness
of the driest soil took the blood of the
challice which suckled each
thread and taste as every tree which
touched with each wrangled root.

Now, well into the cream filled cottony clouds, I shook upon
the crisp cool gasping skies of night as
the breasts you placed before me
warms me in the thighs and wedge of my loins.

I pause and listen to the crickets moan
as the choir of these suckling
chants burrow through the shrubs, bushes and scattered trees,
I angle upon the moisture of the crumbling sky

open as the moisture falling from the freshest
dance of this quivering night.

Darkest

With each step of the tamp of my feet, I swam through the slapping,
pounding wind, loudly yet cleverly alive.

The fine, loose tumbling strands of my
hair gathered the spindling dusts
and gingerly, the sweat of my temples and forehead stretched upon
the glistening wind which burrows the smallest of seeds.

Now, into the depths of the shroud of black, I fall upon the meadow
stout and endless by rows, the stones spoke to me and I trimmed
swiftly beneath the grass and topsoil of the earth.

Clinging, I find the trembling bones and mud which caressed me
as I loosened my breath to the darkest
of shards of the empty mosaic.

Narcissus

I looked upon the lake and watched my
reflection in rippling gushes
of spooling water and gently, the storm swept in passage;
across the thin waters which trembled and danced as the cool air
deepened into the cool clarity of my breath.

I felt the dash of the crumbling waters as every shake from
every gasping wash softened and moistened my face.

With the rise of the sun, I stopped for a
moment and thought of the delicate
smile which opened to the grooves of
the pockets where sweet water
thrusts upon the heat of my face as the
morning crown of the yellow
sun threaded upon me.

I stood, walked into the pine trees and softly
slept upon each fiber and needle.

I breath the cherry blossom as thunder roams the sky.

Birth in the Hollow

The roots of the sycamore swiveled to the deep soils of the ordination
of the newest reach of the earth.

Upon the shade which grew in the earliest bloom of Summer,
I loosened and found the sweat of my
flesh gather across every perch:
stretch of the bridge of my nose, the pastures
of my back, pouch of the roundness
of my belly and the moisture deepened
to the cottons of my aching fee.

Upon the glisten of the nocturnes of the hush of early night,
I stood and walked through the fabric
of the woods and by the depth
of the climb of the chill where satins of the falling sky cooled the
flesh
which glistened on corner and curve, I
walked swiftly into the hollow
where the woods gave birth.

As I Covet

I carve my way through the steep growth of the meadow.
I tamp the sprout of the onion grass with the wind tugging upon
Each threading patch of mint.

Upon reaching the current of the dashing tremble of the creek,
I suckled on the mist which webbed across my tender face.

We met, touched in the stretch of the
rise of the hill which glistened
The hues of green as swiftly, I embraced the dance of the sun
And quivered in the droplets of the moist press, trembling pearls
Of white dew.

I loosened myself upon the breadth of your painted mouth.

I looked upon you and gathered the paleness of your nakedness
As the rise of the thickening press of your tender penis swelled
In all noble faculty and tremor.

With moaning recall, I gathered you in the freshness of the chapel
Where swoons of incense trickled across you.

I covet the pink thrashing angles of the frailty of your body
And breath the scent of the trim cut of your chestnut hair.

Upon the Edge of Night

The posture above the canopy of the spread of the maple tree
rose above the drip of the saps and tossed
shade across the slithering
trail, coated in dust and pebbles and rocks.

Swift, I walked into the depths of the darkening wood as threads
of the mulch and cakes of the cooling,
moisture of the adjoining path
sank upon the gush and throb of the clear hustling creek.

Reaching the open quiver of the meadow and all fondling grass,
I sulked and breathed with the growth as
every dampening blitz of early
morning boasted of perfect soil, flesh of the earth.

The light scattered through the surrounding trees and soft light
blitzed in the moan of the sweeping clouds.

Quietly, I stepped into the endless shade of each endless tree.

Perched on Mountain Ridge

She came to me as I rose beneath the cloth;
I loosened each hem and stitch as the fibers slipped across the pale
quivering flesh I soothed and polished for her.

By the middle of the evening, I took
her by the cup of her palm,
sweetly we stood on the thick wooden patio and looked
upon the hundreds of mountains and entertained the thought
of every ridge and the dash of every mountain creek.

In the moment after the pause of the evenings final touch,
her sweet fragrant hair blossomed within
the eager expansion of my lungs
as my moist mouth soothed the fullness of her breasts.

By morning, she left and hiked to the
perch of the slouching mountain
which gathered an endless gasp of breath.

After the Hike

Winds from the northern mountains
groomed the Wintry fleece of snow
which spooled and sliced across the flat, chilled fields and retreat
of every meadow.

Now, with the current slice and slither
of the heavy gathering of snow,
I walked thigh deep and reached the field of boulders as threads
of my jacket and stretch of my denims held a gnarled glaze.

Reaching the spread of these mountainous
rocks, I held the rays of the sun
as my pale skin stung and cool waters drizzled
across my face, the dampness
of the melting snow caressed me tenderly.

I reached the porch of the wooden dwelling
where I tossed my soaking clothes
and eagerly, I sank within you as the blood
warmed and threaded through me.

Reaching the sauces of your cove, I opened the cake of the earth
and sauntered into the quilts of the earth from which I came.

As the Earth Punishes

I slipped into the heavy cloth which suckled
the sun with all tender blackness.
With the palest collar, I proclaimed of the
softest shade of alabaster, pearl
and the cool stretch of this Winter neck.

I listened as I walk the deep of the country road and gently,
dusts swelled across my pants and sang
my vocalise of sweet lathering
of the swiftness of this country breath.

I begged the swelling gray and charcoal sky to loosen rain upon me
as the steam would rise from the impoverished earth.

I reached the dry cakes of the spiny creek
which lathered the trembling toss
of each dried leaf and the rest of the fallen
branches, crackling in the web of the earth.

Now, the thud and song of the choir of
nightfall cooled each pollen and snap
of the greenest pod.

I fell upon the brown grass and tans of the onion sprouts.
I felt a peeling of my skin and a scream of my wilted flesh.

Well into this madness, I carved my path
through this sting of a bristling depress.

Passing the Threshold

After reaching the threshold of the heaviest
acres of these thick wood,
I listened to the breath of the leaves and
chant of every branch which
reached me in the canvas and treetop.

I dripped in moisture of the breadth of the pounding sunshine
which warmed the forest; I suckled the
milks of this earth and wept
to the fragment of evening scarlet rays which cloaked
the sun within a dash upon the edge of my pale face.

With an open, slither of this pooling,
cool water, I knelt to the bloods
of the soft lulls of this tender Mother and I drank each trickle
from the cream filled breasts on this deserving soil and moisture
which danced with the blooming sky.

By the stretch of night, I wander so happily
through the pulse of the majestic
soothing breath, softly landing upon me.

Stream in the Meadow

With the cup of my soft, soothing palms,
I placed these pouches upon the goblets of her breasts which
held the milk and poised in riddling bloods.

Removing the thin silk of the loosened
blouse which caressed across her
and fell to the cool marble floor,

I paused for a moment and tore the skirt
from her pale white legs and waist;
with the strain of my floundering ears, I listened to the clang
of the bells which told eleven strokes.

I fell to the slither of the stream which pulsed and gushed
through the meadow which fondled and sliced as the cove of her
trembling upper thighs.

Foams swept to the shore in swift eddies and reaching rocks
as I stood naked and dipped through the damp washing waves.

Walking Home

The sky exploded in dark grays and tossed blue ribbons of light
along the weeping soft mud of the earth.

I stood and looked upon her silhouette as
the rhythms of her trembling ghost
wrapped across me in vapors of this lusty phantom
and danced full in this lusty breath of the sweeping storm.

I reach into the burial of my limber palms as the stain of the Book
swelled and reserved the grass in tender
blades and patches of every clover.

The storm loafed to the prisms where each
dash of gray fell to the black
swab and stroke of the night, full of the weeping reach
of the newest moon.

I gathered my things and walked my way home.

Last Stand

I walk along the groove and soft pouches
as they scattered across the earth.
the fine silk threads of your flickering hair cast sweet scents in the
grip of your arrival.

With the removal of your white threaded
shirt, I reached and moaned for
the perch of tender breasts; I drew upon
the quivering beads of your sweat
and soothed each pearl into the cup of each trembling palm.

WIth this moment, I fell to the sprint of the falling sun;
I felt the crusts of the sweet mud cloaked soil as each pasted
blade of grass coddled me in the chyme of this shattered vein.

Last Stand

I walk along the groove and soft pouches
as they scattered across the earth.
the fine silk threads of your flickering hair cast sweet scents in the
grip of your arrival.

With the removal of your white threaded
shirt, I reached and moaned for
the perch of tender breasts; I drew upon
the quivering beads of your sweat
and soothed each pearl into the cup of each trembling palm.

WIth this moment, I fell to the sprint of the falling sun;
I felt the crusts of the sweet mud cloaked soil as each pasted
blade of grass coddled me in the chyme of this shattered vein.

With the sting of the thornbush, I bleed from my lusty flesh.

Lost Beneath the Summer Sun

With the fullness of a murder dashing above,
I hear the 'caw' as the woodland treetops quivered to the shout
Of the hottest moments of the sun.

I, pasted in a relishing sweat, dipped through the endless humidity
Of the fangs of Summer.

Upon reaching the death of the meadow,
my feet filled with the juices
Of Summer and I searched for the creek
which faded only a few years past.

With the divots and grooves of this dusty rock filled earth,
I swept through the cooling sighs of approaching night.

By morning, I reached the patience of
the church door and opened
Upon the rectory as a salve of water trembled across my lips.

Silence After a Walk

With the hustling breath of the sky which
swam in burgundies, pinks
and gentle shades of the whitest wine, my
body loosened to the quivering
spreads of this nocturne which opened my
shirt upon the grooming earth.

In a searing dash of an October moment,
the rains swiped on an angled chill as I felt the refreshing touch
of this suddenly, silent moment.

I loosened these beads from the deep of this pocket and relished,
coveted the trail which led across this ripe, full meadow.

I wandered lost through the endless day
and through the endless night.
awakening from the loft and feathered softness of this depression,
flickering dusts follow my rising flesh as each hustling pasture
swiftly gave way.

Retreat Upon the Sky

Tears fell to the cobblestone floor and
gathered in a trickling pool of blood.
reaching past the rain which gathered and
slapped the edges of the earth
softly glistened in prisms as each thick cloth
swabbed across the perfect statue.

Awake in the threads of murr, I walked the
path to the sweet, empty pews
and knelt in shaking thrusts of sorrow.

I look upon the stained glass and thickened with
warm blood as soft blue spread throughout
the patterns of the room.

Tears shook from the wedge of my closing
eyes and I felt each droplet
disperse across the well chewed edge of my tongue.

In a scurry, light filled the lofting incense
of the emptiness of the church.

I felt the sky subdue.

Graves

I search for the grave of the earth of the
forest floor as the moisture
of the sting and fangs of the dripping
beads; fallen beads gather at the
loosening heels of my feet.

Softly, I carelessly open my shoes and
unbuckle my belt as the slithering
cloth of my pants reaches upon the
slithering walk you bring to me.

Slouching along the rise of the red maple
tree, I absorb into the moist
lull of your fingers and tongue

I watch the sweet girlish figure which slides upon me and I feel the
crash of the broken sky.

In a second, we joust upon the fertile soils by which we soothe.
we awaken and watch the spread of apricot filling the eastern sky.

Mourning Light

I spoke to the gusts and waves of the fog which quavered across
my laced black shoes and rose, crawled across me in eager lust.

The path, I lost beneath me, as the early morning light shook
through the dew thickened leaves.

I looked into the depths of the pale gray hush which spread across
each rigid layer of ground and sweetly,
I levelled my way to the hundreds of mountains
all honoring layers of plateaus
and crests where I slept in solitude.

I awoke to the vapors dripping from her
cloth and slicing with a perfect
smile as the trembling gasp of these warm
hands placed upon my back
and sweetly we embraced as the slender gentle arms of her
kissed the beads of my gushing tears.

Into the light, I endlessly walk, glazed with
the bloods roaming the eastern sky.

Drenched in the hottest sun of madness, she finds me in tenderness.

I sizzled beneath the cloth, I open to the fresh, sweet rain.

Of the last moment of the last morning,
    I find my path leading home.

About the Author

Under and within the landscape of nature, Donny Barilla coats the palate of his metaphoric and imagist reach as he uses the tremble of his pen to wrangle upon the fever of his surroundings which flood and weave each page. Donny motions primarily as a poet and uses techniques such as he writes books of short stories and novellas and searches his creativity in multiple arenas fastened through thought provoking paints which slip from word to page to book. Keeping late hours which sometimes bleeds into the rising patterns of the sun, he works in his study keeping an espresso machine close at hand. Here, he allows the softened press of his discipline, awake and aware at each moment. Having placed ninety-four poems in journals and magazines, he also donated twenty three books to libraries, academic and public. Donny took first place in the Adelaide Literary Award for Poetry and has placed on two other occasions. After building a construct of vowels and consonants, the words blend upon the page as he pays due respect to the motions of the English language and passions of poetic touch.

www.ingramcontent.com/pod-product-compliance
Lightning Source LLC
Chambersburg PA
CBHW032230080426
42735CB00008B/792